PIANO · VOCAL · GUITAR

TOP HITS OF 2008

ISBN 978-1-4234-6134-0

HAL•LEONARD® CORPORATION

7777 W. BLUEMOUND RD. P.O. BOX 13819 MILWAUKEE, WI 53213

Visit Hal Leonard Online at
www.halleonard.com

CONTENTS

BLEEDING LOVE

Words and Music by JESSE McCARTNEY
and RYAN TEDDER

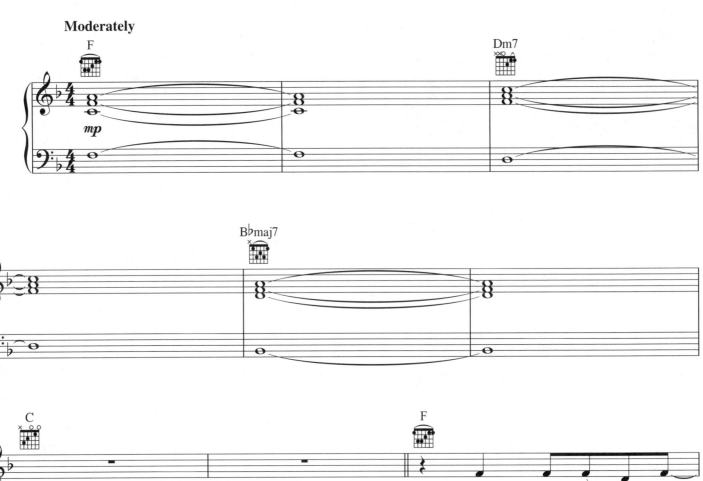

DON'T STOP THE MUSIC

Words and Music by TOR ERIK HERMANSEN
FRANKIE STORM, MIKKEL ERIKSEN
and MICHAEL JACKSON

Moderately fast Dance groove

FEELS LIKE TONIGHT

Words and Music by SHEP SOLOMON,
MARTIN SANDBERG and LUKASZ GOTTWALD

Recorded a half step lower.

FINALLY

Words and Music by STACY FERGUSON,
JOHN STEPHENS and STEFANIE RIDEL

Tender Ballad

Ev - er since I was a ba - by girl, I had a dream,
I re - mem - ber the be - gin - ning, you al - read - y knew, I

Cin - der - el - la theme, cra - zy as it seems.
act - ed like a fool, just try - ing to be cool.

Al - ways knew that deep in - side that there would come that day, but
Front - ing like it did - n't mat - ter, I just ran a - way, put

I would have to wait, make so man - y mis - takes.
on an - oth - er face, was lost in my own space.

I KISSED A GIRL

Words and Music by CATHY DENNIS,
MAX MARTIN, LUKASZ GOTTWALD
and KATY PERRY

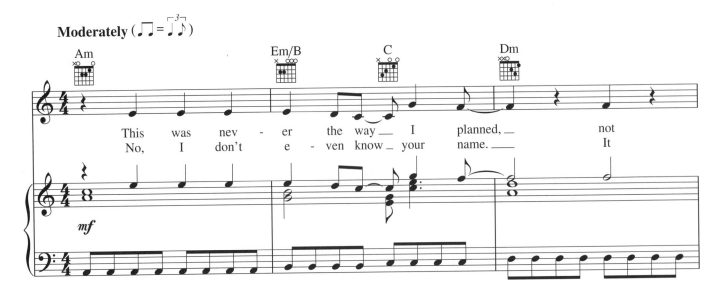

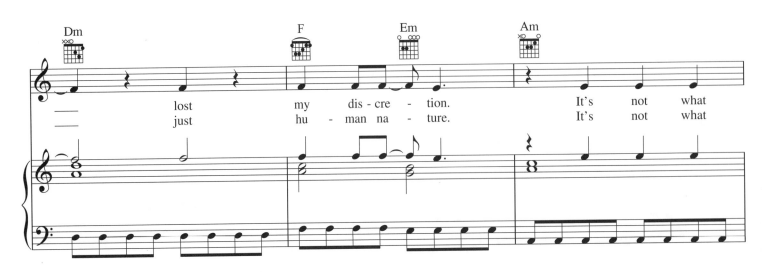

IT'S NOT MY TIME

Words and Music by BRAD ARNOLD, ROBERT HARRELL,
CHRISTOPHER HENDERSON and MATTHEW ROBERTS

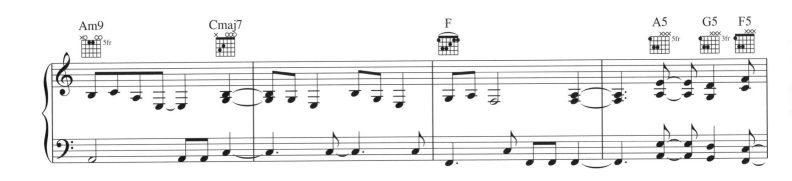

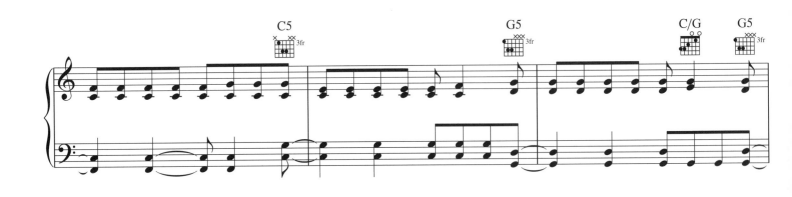

LEAVIN'

Words and Music by CORRON COLE,
CHRISTOPHER STEWART, TERIUS NASH
and JAMES BUNTON

Moderate groove

LOST

Words and Music by JANN ARDEN RICHARDS,
MICHAEL BUBLÉ and ALAN CHANG

Recorded a half step lower.

LOVE SONG

Words and Music by
SARA BAREILLES

MERCY

Words and Music by AIMEE DUFFY
and STEPHEN BOOKER

_____ me? I'm beg - ging you for mer - cy,

you got me beg - ging, you got me beg - ging, you got me beg - ging...

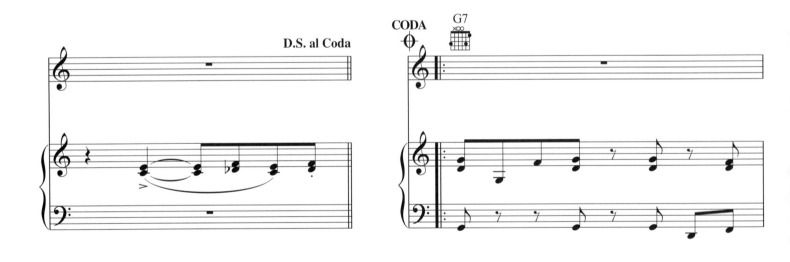

D.S. al Coda

CODA G7

Repeat ad lib. to Fade

Beg-ging you for mer - cy, you got me beg - ging, down on my knees, I said...

NO AIR

Words and Music by JAMES FAUNTLEROY II,
STEVEN RUSSELL, HARVEY MASON, JR.,
DAMON THOMAS and ERIK GRIGGS

Moderately

Female: Tell me how I'm s'posed to breathe with no air, air, air.

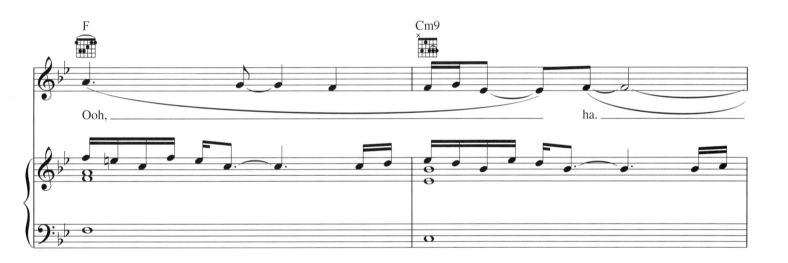

Ooh, ha.

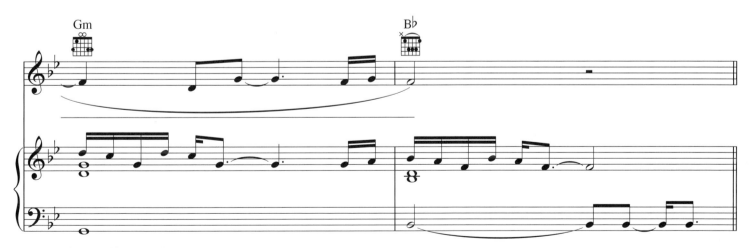

* *Recorded a half step higher.*

POCKETFUL OF SUNSHINE

Words and Music by NATASHA BEDINGFIELD,
DANIELLE BRISEBOIS and JOHN SHANKS

REALIZE

Words and Music by COLBIE CAILLAT,
JASON REEVES and MIKAL BLUE

*Recorded a half step higher.
Guitarists: Capo at 6th fret to play along with recording.

SEE YOU AGAIN

Words and Music by DESTINY HOPE CYRUS,
TIM JAMES and ANTONINA ARMATO

STOP AND STARE

Words and Music by RYAN TEDDER,
ANDREW BROWN, TIM MYERS,
ZACK FILKINS and EDDIE FISHER

TAKE A BOW

Words and Music by SHAFFER SMITH,
TOR ERIK HERMANSEN and MIKKEL ERIKSEN

VIVA LA VIDA

Words and Music by GUY BERRYMAN, JON BUCKLAND,
WILL CHAMPION and CHRIS MARTIN

WHEN I GROW UP

Words and Music by JIM McCARTY,
PAUL SAMWELL-SMITH, RODNEY JERKINS,
THERON THOMAS and TIMOTHY THOMAS

WHEN YOU LOOK ME IN THE EYES

Words and Music by NICHOLAS JONAS,
JOSEPH JONAS, KEVIN JONAS II, KEVIN JONAS SR.,
RAYMOND BOYD and PJ BIANCO

If the heart is al - ways search - ing, can you ev - er find _ a home?
How long will I _ be wait - ing to be with you _ a - gain? _

_ I've been look - ing for _ that some - one; I'll nev - er make it on _ my own. _
_ I'm gon - na tell you that _ I love _ you in the best way that _ I can. _

WITH YOU

Words and Music by TOR ERIK HERMANSEN,
ESPEN LIND, AMUND BJORKLUND,
MIKKEL ERIKSEN and JOHNTA AUSTIN

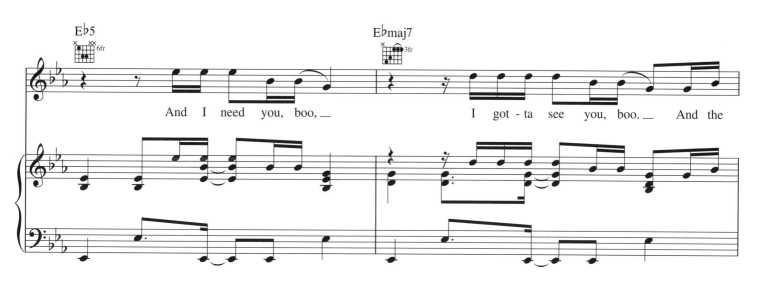

133

WON'T GO HOME WITHOUT YOU

Words and Music by
ADAM LEVINE

Moderate Rock

I asked her to stay ___ but she would-n't lis-

ten, and she left ___ be-fore ___ I had ___
ver, and the nois - es that ___ you made ___

the chance ___ to say, ___ oh, ___ the
kept me ___ a - wake, ___ oh. ___ The

HAL·LEONARD ESSENTIAL SONGS

Play the best songs from the Roaring '20s to today! Each collection features dozens of the most memorable songs of each decade, or in your favorite musical style, arranged in piano/vocal/guitar format.

THE 1920s
Over 100 songs that shaped the decade: Ain't We Got Fun? • Basin Street Blues • Bye Bye Blackbird • Can't Help Lovin' Dat Man • I Wanna Be Loved by You • Makin' Whoopee • Ol' Man River • Puttin' On the Ritz • Toot, Toot, Tootsie • Yes Sir, That's My Baby • and more.
00311200 ....$24.95

THE 1930s
97 essential songs from the 1930s: April in Paris • Body and Soul • Cheek to Cheek • Falling in Love with Love • Georgia on My Mind • Heart and Soul • I'll Be Seeing You • The Lady Is a Tramp • Mood Indigo • My Funny Valentine • You Are My Sunshine • and more.
00311193 ....$24.95

THE 1940s
An amazing collection of over 100 songs from the '40s: Boogie Woogie Bugle Boy • Don't Get Around Much Anymore • Have I Told You Lately That I Love You • I'll Remember April • Route 66 • Sentimental Journey • Take the "A" Train • You'd Be So Nice to Come Home To • and more.
00311192 ....$24.95

THE 1950s
Over 100 pivotal songs from the 1950s, including: All Shook Up • Bye Bye Love • Chantilly Lace • Fever • Great Balls of Fire • Kansas City • Love and Marriage • Mister Sandman • Rock Around the Clock • Sixteen Tons • Tennessee Waltz • Wonderful! Wonderful! • and more.
00311191 ....$24.95

THE 1960s
104 '60s essentials, including: Baby Love • California Girls • Dancing in the Street • Hey Jude • I Heard It Through the Grapevine • Respect • Stand by Me • Twist and Shout • Will You Love Me Tomorrow • Yesterday • You Keep Me Hangin' On • and more.
00311190 ....$24.95

THE 1970s
Over 80 of the best songs from the '70s: American Pie • Band on the Run • Come Sail Away • Dust in the Wind • I Feel the Earth Move • Let It Be • Morning Has Broken • Smoke on the Water • Take a Chance on Me • The Way We Were • You're So Vain • and more.
00311189 ....$24.95

THE 1980s
Over 70 classics from the age of power pop and hair metal: Against All Odds • Call Me • Ebony and Ivory • The Heat Is On • Jump • Manic Monday • Sister Christian • Time After Time • Up Where We Belong • What's Love Got to Do with It • and more.
00311188 ....$24.95

THE 1990s
68 songs featuring country-crossover, swing revival, the birth of grunge, and more: Change the World • Fields of Gold • Ironic • Livin' La Vida Loca • More Than Words • Smells like Teen Spirit • Walking in Memphis • Zoot Suit Riot • and more.
00311187 ....$24.95

THE 2000s
59 of the best songs that brought in the new millennium: Accidentally in Love • Beautiful • Don't Know Why • Get the Party Started • Hey Ya! • I Hope You Dance • 1985 • This Love • A Thousand Miles • Wherever You Will Go • Who Let the Dogs Out • You Raise Me Up • and more.
00311186.................................$24.95

ACOUSTIC ROCK
Over 70 songs, including: About a Girl • Barely Breathing • Blowin' in the Wind • Fast Car • I Want to Know What Love Is • Landslide • Sunshine on My Shoulders • Turn! Turn! Turn! (To Everything There Is a Season) • Walk on the Wild Side • and more.
00311747.................................$24.95

THE BEATLES
Over 90 of the finest from this extraordinary band: All My Loving • Back in the U.S.S.R. • Blackbird • Come Together • Get Back • Help! • Hey Jude • If I Fell • Let It Be • Michelle • Penny Lane • Something • Twist and Shout • Yesterday • more!
00311389.................................$24.95

BROADWAY
Over 90 songs of the stage: Any Dream Will Do • Blue Skies • Cabaret • Don't Cry for Me, Argentina • Edelweiss • Hello, Dolly! • I'll Be Seeing You • Memory • The Music of the Night • Oklahoma • Summer Nights • There's No Business Like Show Business • Tomorrow • more.
00311222.................................$24.95

CHRISTMAS
Over 100 essential holiday favorites: Blue Christmas • The Christmas Song • Deck the Hall • Frosty the Snow Man • Joy to the World • Merry Christmas, Darling • Rudolph the Red-Nosed Reindeer • Silver Bells • and more!
00311241.................................$24.95

COUNTRY
96 essential country standards, including: Achy Breaky Heart • Crazy • The Devil Went down to Georgia • Elvira • Friends in Low Places • God Bless the U.S.A. • Here You Come Again • Lucille • Redneck Woman • Tennessee Waltz • and more.
00311296.................................$24.95

JAZZ STANDARDS
99 jazz classics no music library should be without: Autumn in New York • Body and Soul • Don't Get Around Much Anymore • Easy to Love (You'd Be So Easy to Love) • I've Got You Under My Skin • The Lady Is a Tramp • Mona Lisa • Satin Doll • Stardust • Witchcraft • and more.
00311226 ....$24.95

LOVE SONGS
Over 80 romantic hits: Can You Feel the Love Tonight • Endless Love • From This Moment On • Have I Told You Lately • I Just Called to Say I Love You • Love Will Keep Us Together • My Heart Will Go On • Wonderful Tonight • You Are So Beautiful • more.
00311235 ....$24.95

LOVE STANDARDS
100 romantic standards: Dream a Little Dream of Me • The Glory of Love • I Left My Heart in San Francisco • I've Got My Love to Keep Me Warm • The Look of Love • A Time for Us • You Are the Sunshine of My Life • and more.
00311256 ....$24.95

MOVIE SONGS
94 of the most popular silver screen songs: Alfie • Beauty and the Beast • Chariots of Fire • Footloose • I Will Remember You • Jailhouse Rock • Moon River • People • Somewhere Out There • Summer Nights • Unchained Melody • and more.
00311236 ....$24.95

ROCK
Over 80 essential rock classics: Black Magic Woman • Day Tripper • Free Bird • A Groovy Kind of Love • I Shot the Sheriff • The Joker • My Sharona • Oh, Pretty Woman • Proud Mary • Rocket Man • Roxanne • Takin' Care of Business • A Whiter Shade of Pale • Wild Thing • more!
00311390 ....$24.95

TV SONGS
Over 100 terrific tube tunes, including: The Addams Family Theme • Bonanza • The Brady Bunch • Desperate Housewives Main Title • I Love Lucy • Law and Order • Linus and Lucy • Sesame Street Theme • Theme from the Simpsons • Theme from the X-Files • and more!
00311223 ....$24.95

WEDDING
83 songs of love and devotion: All I Ask of You • Canon in D • Don't Know Much • Endless Love • Here, There and Everywhere • Love Me Tender • My Heart Will Go On • Somewhere Out There • Wedding March • You Raise Me Up • and more.
00311309 P/V/G.................................$24.95

FOR MORE INFORMATION, SEE YOUR LOCAL MUSIC DEALER, OR WRITE TO:

HAL·LEONARD® CORPORATION
7777 W. BLUEMOUND RD. P.O. BOX 13819 MILWAUKEE, WI 53213

Complete contents listings are available online at **www.halleonard.com**

Prices, contents and availability subject to change without notice.

0308

THE ULTIMATE SONGBOOKS

These great songbook/CD packs come with our standard arrangements for piano and voice with guitar chord frames plus a CD.
The CD includes a full performance of each song, as well as a second track without the piano part so you can play "lead" with the band!

Vol. 1 Movie Music
00311072 P/V/G.....................$14.95

Vol. 2 Jazz Ballads
00311073 P/V/G.....................$14.95

Vol. 3 Timeless Pop
00311074 P/V/G.....................$14.95

Vol. 4 Broadway Classics
00311075 P/V/G.....................$14.95

Vol. 5 Disney
00311076 P/V/G.....................$14.95

**Vol. 6
Country Standards**
00311077 P/V/G.....................$14.95

Vol. 7 Love Songs
00311078 P/V/G.....................$14.95

Vol. 8 Classical Themes
00311079 Piano Solo..............$14.95

Vol. 9 Children's Songs
0311080 P/V/G.....................$14.95

Vol. 10 Wedding Classics
00311081 Piano Solo..............$14.95

**Vol. 11
Wedding Favorites**
00311097 P/V/G.....................$14.95

**Vol. 12
Christmas Favorites**
00311137 P/V/G.....................$14.95

**Vol. 13
Yuletide Favorites**
00311138 P/V/G.....................$14.95

Vol. 14 Pop Ballads
00311145 P/V/G.....................$14.95

**Vol. 15
Favorite Standards**
00311146 P/V/G.....................$14.95

Vol. 16 TV Classics
00311147 P/V/G.....................$14.95

Vol. 17 Movie Favorites
00311148 P/V/G.....................$14.95

Vol. 18 Jazz Standards
00311149 P/V/G.....................$14.95

**Vol. 19
Contemporary Hits**
00311162 P/V/G.....................$14.95

Vol. 20 R&B Ballads
00311163 P/V/G.....................$14.95

Vol. 21 Big Band
00311164 P/V/G.....................$14.95

Vol. 22 Rock Classics
00311165 P/V/G.....................$14.95

Vol. 23 Worship Classics
00311166 P/V/G.....................$14.95

Vol. 24 Les Misérables
00311169 P/V/G.....................$14.95

**Vol. 25
The Sound of Music**
00311175 P/V/G.....................$14.95

**Vol. 26 Andrew Lloyd
Webber Favorites**
00311178 P/V/G.....................$14.95

**Vol. 27 Andrew Lloyd
Webber Greats**
00311179 P/V/G.....................$14.95

**Vol. 28
Lennon & McCartney**
00311180 P/V/G.....................$14.95

Vol. 29 The Beach Boys
00311181 P/V/G.....................$14.95

Vol. 30 Elton John
00311182 P/V/G.....................$14.95

Vol. 31 Carpenters
00311183 P/V/G.....................$14.95

**Vol. 32
Bacharach & David**
00311218 P/V/G.....................$14.95

Vol. 33 Peanuts™
00311227 P/V/G.....................$14.95

**Vol. 34 Charlie Brown
Christmas**
00311228 P/V/G.....................$14.95

**Vol. 35
Elvis Presley Hits**
00311230 P/V/G.....................$14.95

**Vol. 36
Elvis Presley Greats**
00311231 P/V/G.....................$14.95

**Vol. 37 Contemporary
Christian**
00311232 P/V/G.....................$14.95

**Vol. 38 Duke Ellington –
Standards**
00311233 P/V/G.....................$14.95

**Vol. 39 Duke Ellington –
Classics**
00311234 P/V/G.....................$14.95

Vol. 40 Showtunes
00311237 P/V/G.....................$14.95

**Vol. 41
Rodgers & Hammerstein**
00311238 P/V/G.....................$14.95

Vol. 42 Irving Berlin
00311339 P/V/G.....................$14.95

Vol. 43 Jerome Kern
00311340 P/V/G.....................$14.95

**Vol. 44 Frank Sinatra –
Popular Hits**
00311377 P/V/G.....................$14.95

**Vol. 45 Frank Sinatra –
Most Requested Songs**
00311378 P/V/G.....................$14.95

Vol. 46 Wicked
00311317 P/V/G.....................$14.95

Vol. 47 Rent
00311319 P/V/G.....................$14.95

**Vol. 48
Christmas Carols**
00311332 P/V/G.....................$14.95

Vol. 49 Holiday Hits
00311333 P/V/G.....................$14.95

**Vol. 51
High School Musical**
00311421 P/V/G.....................$19.95

**Vol. 52 Andrew Lloyd
Webber Classics**
00311422 P/V/G.....................$14.95

Vol. 53 Grease
00311450 P/V/G.....................$14.95

**Vol. 54
Broadway Favorites**
00311451 P/V/G.....................$14.95

Vol. 55 The 1940s
00311453 P/V/G.....................$14.95

Vol. 56 The 1950s
00311459 P/V/G.....................$14.95

**Vol. 63
High School Musical 2**
00311470 P/V/G.....................$19.95

**Vol. 64
God Bless America**
00311489 P/V/G.....................$14.95

Vol. 65 Casting Crowns
00311494 P/V/G.....................$14.95

FOR MORE INFORMATION, SEE YOUR LOCAL MUSIC DEALER,
OR WRITE TO:

**HAL•LEONARD®
CORPORATION**

7777 W. BLUEMOUND RD. P.O. BOX 13819 MILWAUKEE, WI 53213

Visit Hal Leonard Online at **www.halleonard.com**

Prices, contents, and availability subject to change without notice.
Disney characters and artwork © Disney Enterprises, Inc.

Pro Vocal® Series
SONGBOOK & SOUND-ALIKE CD
SING 8 CHART-TOPPING SONGS WITH A PROFESSIONAL BAND

Whether you're a karaoke singer or an auditioning professional, the Pro Vocal® series is for you! Unlike most karaoke packs, each book in the ProVocal Series contains the lyrics, melody, and chord symbols for eight hit songs. The CD contains demos for listening, and separate backing tracks so you can sing along. The CD is playable on any CD player, but it is also enhanced so PC and Mac computer users can adjust the recording to any pitch without changing the tempo! Perfect for home rehearsal, parties, auditions, corporate events, and gigs without a backup band.

BROADWAY SONGS
00740247 Women's Edition.....................................$12.95
00740248 Men's Edition...$12.95

MICHAEL BUBLÉ
00740362 Men's Edition...$14.95

CHRISTMAS HITS
00740396 Women's Edition.....................................$14.95
00740397 Men's Edition...$14.95

CHRISTMAS STANDARDS
00740299 Women's Edition.....................................$12.95
00740298 Men's Edition...$12.95

KELLY CLARKSON
00740377 Women's Edition.....................................$14.95

PATSY CLINE
00740374 Women's Edition.....................................$14.95

CONTEMPORARY CHRISTIAN
00740390 Women's Edition.....................................$14.95
00740391 Men's Edition...$14.95

CONTEMPORARY HITS
00740246 Women's Edition.....................................$12.95
00740251 Men's Edition...$12.95

MILEY CYRUS
00740394 Women's Edition.....................................$14.95

DISCO FEVER
00740281 Women's Edition.....................................$12.95
00740282 Men's Edition...$12.95

DISNEY'S BEST
00740344 Women's Edition.....................................$14.95
00740345 Men's Edition...$14.95

DISNEY FAVORITES
00740342 Women's Edition.....................................$14.95
00740343 Men's Edition...$14.95

'80S GOLD
00740277 Women's Edition.....................................$12.95
00740278 Men's Edition...$12.95

ELLA FITZGERALD
00740378 Women's Edition.....................................$14.95

GREASE
00740369 Women's Edition.....................................$14.95
00740370 Men's Edition...$14.95

JOSH GROBAN
00740371 Men's Edition...$17.95

HAIRSPRAY
00740379 Women's Edition.....................................$14.95

HANNAH MONTANA
00740375 Girl's Edition...$14.95

MORE HANNAH MONTANA
00740393 Girl's Edition...$14.95

HIGH SCHOOL MUSICAL 1 & 2
00740360 Women's Edition.....................................$14.95
00740361 Guy's Edition...$14.95

HIP-HOP HITS
00740368 Men's Edition...$14.95

HITS OF THE '50S
00740381 Men's Edition...$14.95

HITS OF THE '60S
00740382 Men's Edition...$14.95

HITS OF THE '70S
00740384 Women's Edition.....................................$14.95
00740383 Men's Edition $14.95

BILLIE HOLIDAY
00740388 Women's Edition.....................................$14.95

JAZZ BALLADS
00740353 Women's Edition.....................................$12.95

JAZZ FAVORITES
00740354 Women's Edition.....................................$12.95

Prices, contents, & availability subject to change without notice.
Disney charaters and artwork © Disney Enterprises, Inc.

JAZZ STANDARDS
00740249 Women's Edition.....................................$12.95
00740250 Men's Edition...$12.95

JAZZ VOCAL STANDARDS
0074037 Women's Edition.......................................$14.95

BILLY JOEL
00740373 Men's Edition...$17.95

MOVIE SONGS
00740365 Women's Edition.....................................$14.95
00740366 Men's Edition...$14.95

MUSICALS OF BOUBLIL & SCHÖNBERG
00740350 Women's Edition.....................................$14.95
00740351 Men's Edition...$14.95

ELVIS PRESLEY
00740333 Volume 1 ....$14.95
00740335 Volume 2 ....$14.95

R&B SUPER HITS
00740279 Women's Edition.....................................$12.95
00740280 Men's Edition...$12.95

FRANK SINATRA CLASSICS
00740347 Men's Edition...$14.95

FRANK SINATRA STANDARDS
00740346 Men's Edition...$14.95

THE SOUND OF MUSIC
00740389 Women's Edition.....................................$14.95

TORCH SONGS
00740363 Women's Edition.....................................$12.95
00740364 Men's Edition...$12.95

TOP HITS
00740380 Women's Edition.....................................$14.95

VOCAL WARM-UPS
00740395 ....$14.95

ANDREW LLOYD WEBBER
00740348 Women's Edition.....................................$14.95
00740349 Men's Edition...$14.95

WEDDING GEMS
00740309 Book/CD Pack Women's Edition $12.95
00740310 Book/CD Pack Men's Edition $12.95
00740311 Duets Edition...$12.95

WICKED
00740392 Women's Edition.....................................$14.95

HANK WILLIAMS
00740386 Men's Edition...$14.95

0608

Visit Hal Leonard online at www.halleonard.com